KHRUSHCHEV

COLORING BOOK

[*By Appointment to H. R. H. Czar Nicholas II*]

Conceived and Written by

GENE SHALIT

Drawings by

JACK DAVIS

Courageous Publisher

ARNOLD E. ABRAMSON

Vice Commissar For Forced Sales

ROBERT J. ABRAMSON

Art Commissar

FRANC L. ROGGERI

Banned in

BULGARIA, RUMANIA, ALBANIA, ESTONIA, LAVIA, LITHUANIA,

HUNGARIA, CUBIA, SIBERIA, and SHMETINIA

Dropped into Russia by

KABLE NEWS COMPANY U-2 PLANES

Khrushchev's Top Secret Coloring Book originally published by Universal Publishing and Distributing Corporation, November, 1962.

ISBN: 978-1-936404-63-6
Published July, 2016 by About Comics, Camarillo, California. www.AboutComics.com

For bulk orders, custom covers, or other inquiries, contact *questions@aboutcomics.com*

This is my mother. This is my father.
There are my three sisters. Here are
my brothers. See my neighbors. See
their six children. See my other
neighbors. See their children. What
a big group we are! We all live in
the same room.

See our family.
We are going to spend our vacation
at my Grandmother's.
How we are looking forward to it!
My Grandmother lives in our cellar.

VULGER BOATMAN

See our radio.
It has such a big dial.
How many numbers it has!
How come it gets only one station?

This is the Moscow Stadium.
The teams are playing for the soccer championship.
Today we are playing Albania.
We do not care if we win or lose.
What counts is sportsmanship.
Color the Albanian's skull red.

This is the courtroom in our village.
See the jury.
See the judge.
They have heard all the evidence.
The case is complete.
But they have not given their verdict.
They are waiting for the messenger to
come with the envelope from Moscow.

There is the Press Secretary of the USA.
He is skeet shooting with our Leader.
The Press Secretary is very smart.
He does not let our Leader get behind him.

See the six members of the Politburo.
They have all had heart attacks.
Splatter the wall red.

See our glorious amateur athletes.
They are preparing for the Olympics.
How happy they are!
They are well paid.

See our glorious inventors.
That man is inventing the telephone.
The other man is inventing the wheel.
See the third man.
He is waiting for our embassy in Washington
to send in this week's patents.

See the Great Banquet Hall of the Kremlin.
We are honoring our glorious Chinese allies.
They are studying the menu.
They can't decide between list A and list B.
How friendly everyone is.
Hail to the peace-loving peoples' democracies!
Only one glorious ally is not in this room.

We could never have a banquet without him.

He ... is ... in ... the ....

KREMLIN KITCHEN

............kitchen.

See the big hole.
It is fourteen miles wide and seven miles deep.
It was Kievograd.
Our underground atomic scientists miscalculated.
Color their faces red.

This is our collective farm.
We grow corn.
Our leader visited us last week.
Next year there will be more corn to eat.
After he left there were fewer people.

See the donkey.
Hello, donkey.
He works in the fields.
He is seventeen years old.
His name is "Tractor."
We have more tractors than
any other country in the world.

Our collective has a library.
It has many history books.
They faithfully record the past events
of our glorious country.
I wonder why our history books are loose leaf.

Here are members of our glorious diplomatic corps.
They will go to many countries as peaceful
envoys of the people.
They have all graduated from spy school.

This is a line.
Our glorious country is filled with lines.
Some lines are for stores.
Some are for Lenin's tomb.
We have been standing in this line for three hours.
I wonder what this line is for.

How happy my father is!
Mother has just had a baby.
We have not seen our new baby yet.
We will see it when our mother comes in
from ploughing the fields.

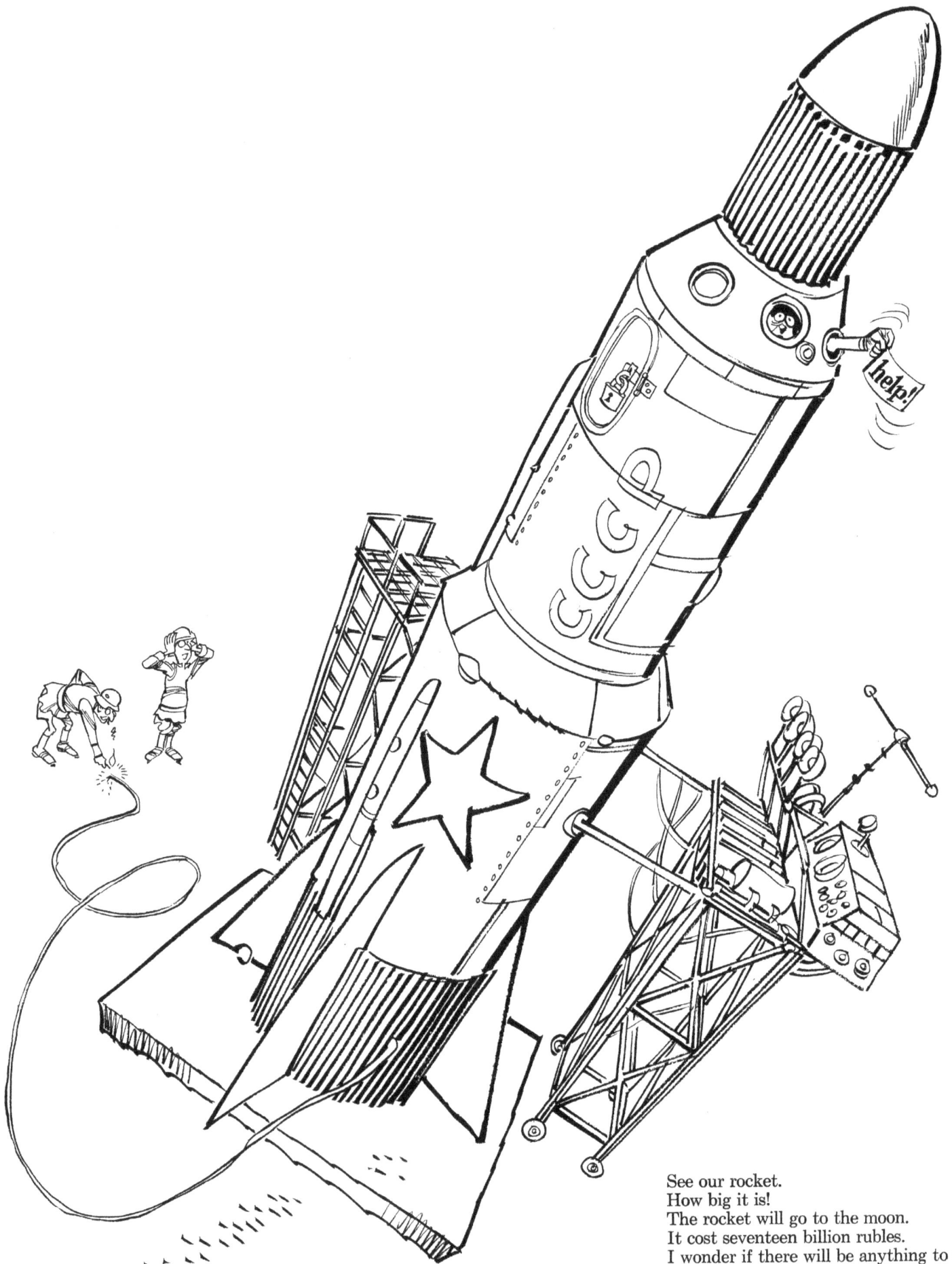

See our rocket.
How big it is!
The rocket will go to the moon.
It cost seventeen billion rubles.
I wonder if there will be anything to eat
when I get home tonight.

This is the document room in the Kremlin.
Our treaties are written here.
See our Director of Treaties.
He has won the Order of Lenin.
He invented disappearing ink.

See our leader.
He is leaving for the United Nations.
He will be there three weeks.
He is taking one suit.
He is taking one shirt.
He is taking three shoes.
Two are for wearing.
One is for pounding.

www.ingramcontent.com/pod-product-compliance
Lightning Source LLC
Chambersburg PA
CBHW080538030426
42337CB00023B/4783